Music Theory Practice Paper 2021 Grade 2 A
Model Answers

1 Rhythm

1.1 (a) $\mathbf{\frac{3}{4}}$ (3)

(b) $\mathbf{\frac{4}{4}}$

(c) $\mathbf{\frac{3}{2}}$

1.2 (5)

1.3 (a) 4 (2)

(b) 6

1.4 (1)

1.5   (3)

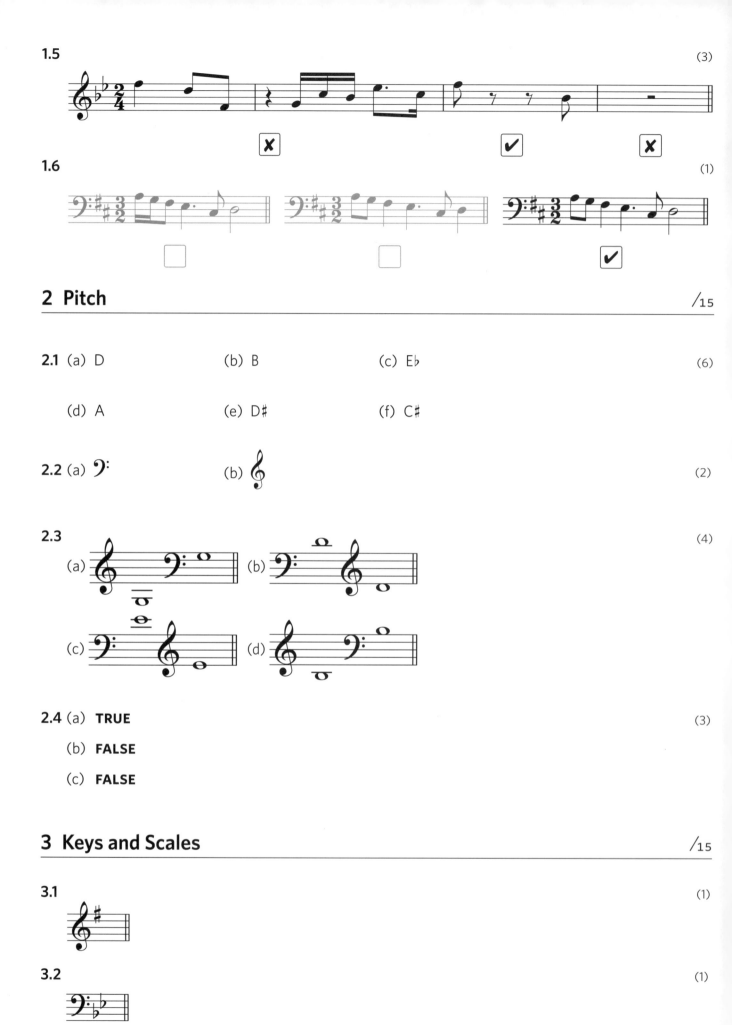

1.6   (1)

2 Pitch   /15

2.1 (a) D   (b) B   (c) E♭   (6)

(d) A   (e) D♯   (f) C♯

2.2 (a) 𝄢   (b) 𝄞   (2)

2.3   (4)

(a)   (b)

(c)   (d)

2.4 (a) **TRUE**   (3)

(b) **FALSE**

(c) **FALSE**

3 Keys and Scales   /15

3.1   (1)

3.2   (1)

3.3 (3)

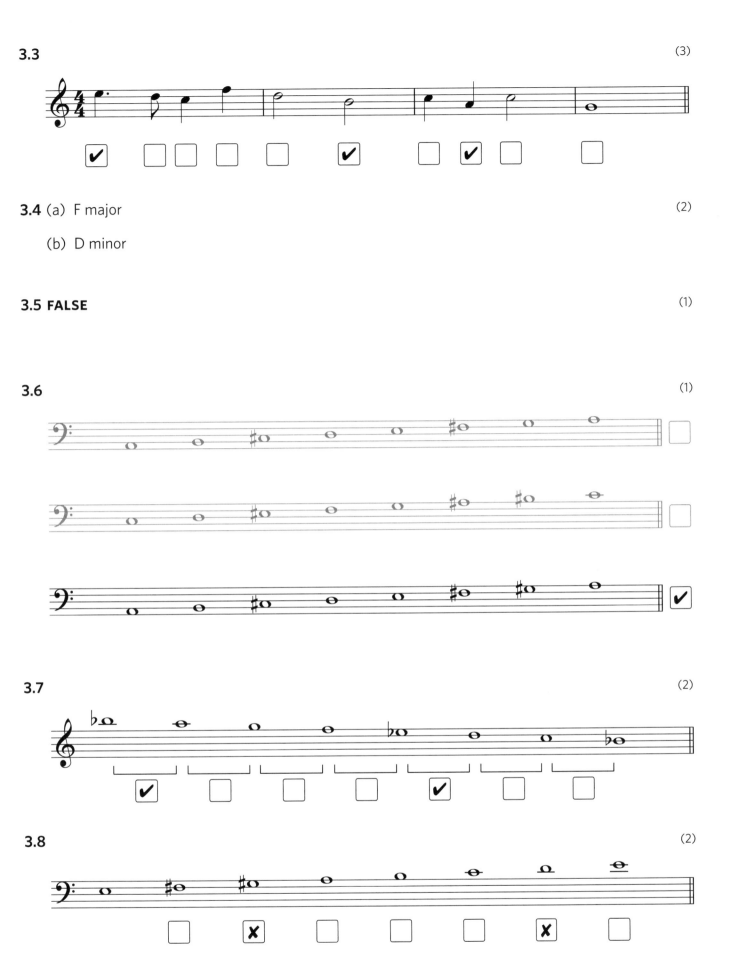

3.4 (a) F major (2)

(b) D minor

3.5 FALSE (1)

3.6 (1)

3.7 (2)

3.8 (2)

3.9 X C♯ (2)

Y E

4 Intervals

/10

(a) 6th   (b) 8th/8ve   (c) 4th   (10)

(d) 5th   (e) 3rd   (f) 2nd

(g) 7th   (h) 8th/8ve   (i) 2nd

(j) 6th

5 Tonic Triads

/10

5.1 (a) **TRUE**   (2)

   (b) **FALSE**

5.2   (3)

(a)  (b)  (c)

5.3 (a) C major   (5)

   (b) E♭ major

   (c) B♭ major

   (d) A minor

   (e) D major

6 Terms, Signs and Instruments /5

♩ = 88 means:

88 crotchet beats in a minute

Largo means:

slow, stately

pp means:

very quiet

(5)

grazioso means:

graceful

Allargando means:

broadening

7 Music in Context /5

7.1 FALSE (1)

7.2 bar 1 (1)

7.3 (a) bar 8 (3)

(b) bar 3

(c) D

Music Theory Practice Paper 2021 Grade 2 B
Model Answers

1 Rhythm

1.1 (a) $\frac{3}{2}$ (3)

(b) $\frac{3}{4}$

(c) $\frac{4}{4}$

1.2   (5)

1.3 (a) 8   (2)

(b) 6

1.4   (1)

1.5 (3)

                ✗   ✔   ✗

1.6 (1)

     ☐   ✔   ☐

2 Pitch /15

2.1 (a) C♯   (b) B♭   (c) G♯   (6)

    (d) A♭   (e) F   (f) E

2.2 (a) 𝄞   (b) 𝄢   (2)

2.3 (4)

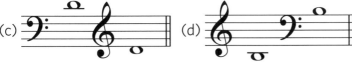

2.4 (a) **TRUE** (3)

    (b) **FALSE**

    (c) **TRUE**

3 Keys and Scales /15

3.1 (1)

3.2 (1)

3.3 (3)

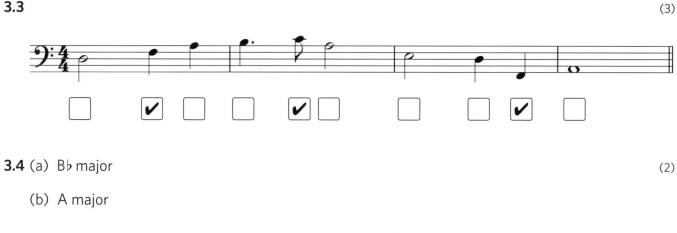

3.4 (a) B♭ major (2)

(b) A major

3.5 TRUE (1)

3.6 (1)

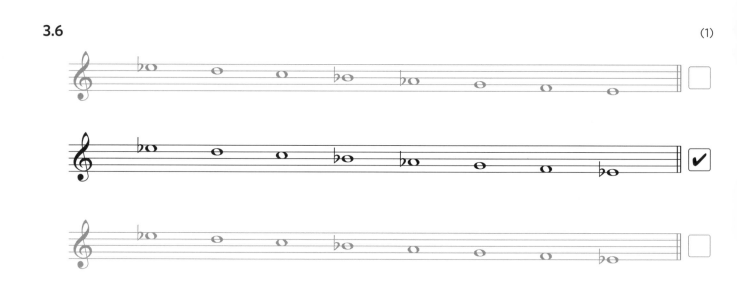

3.7 (2)

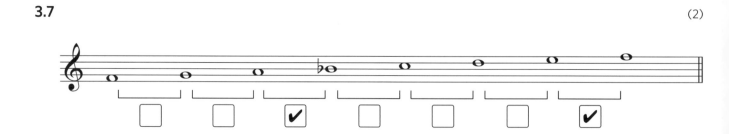

3.8 (2)

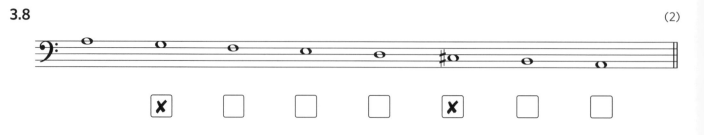

3.9 X E♭ (2)

Y C

4 Intervals /10

(a) 2nd   (b) 8th/8ve   (c) 3rd   (10)

(d) 7th   (e) 6th   (f) 5th

(g) 4th   (h) 7th   (i) 2nd

(j) 5th

5 Tonic Triads /10

5.1 (a) **FALSE**   (2)

   (b) **FALSE**

5.2   (3)

  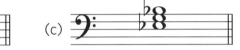

5.3 (a) A major   (5)

   (b) E minor

   (c) D major

   (d) B♭ major

   (e) A minor

6 Terms, Signs and Instruments   /5

fp means:

loud, then immediately soft

⌢ means:

pause on the note or rest

Grave means: (5)

very slow, solemn

dolce means:

sweet

Molto means:

very, much

7 Music in Context   /5

7.1 FALSE   (1)

7.2 bar 8   (1)

7.3 (a) bar 6   (3)

    (b) bar 3

    (c) C♯

Music Theory Practice Paper 2021 Grade 2 C
Model Answers

1 Rhythm
/15

1.1 (a) $\frac{2}{4}$
(3)

(b) $\frac{2}{2}$

(c) $\frac{3}{2}$

1.2
(5)

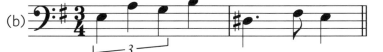

1.3 (a) 6
(2)

(b) 4

1.4
(1)

1.5 (3)

1.6 (1)

2 Pitch /15

2.1 (a) G (b) C♯ (c) E♭ (6)

(d) B (e) C (f) B♭

2.2 (a) 𝄢 (b) 𝄞 (2)

2.3 (4)

(a) (b)

(c) (d)

2.4 (a) **FALSE** (3)

(b) **FALSE**

(c) **TRUE**

3 Keys and Scales /15

3.1 (1)

3.2 (1)

3.3 (3)

3.4 (a) D minor (2)

(b) A major

3.5 TRUE (1)

3.6 (1)

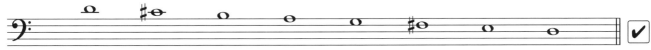

3.7 (2)

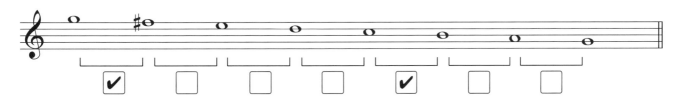

3.8 (2)

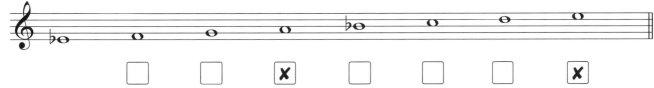

3.9 X D♯ (2)

Y G

4 Intervals

/10

(a) 5th   (b) 4th   (c) 2nd   (10)

(d) 5th   (e) 6th   (f) 4th

(g) 7th   (h) 8th/8ve   (i) 3rd

(j) 5th

5 Tonic Triads

/10

5.1 (a) **FALSE**   (2)

(b) **TRUE**

5.2   (3)

(a) 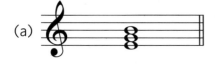   (b) 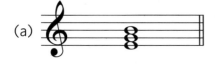   (c)

5.3 (a) D major   (5)

(b) G major

(c) C major

(d) B♭ major

(e) A minor

6 Terms, Signs and Instruments /5

al fine means: **ritenuto** means: ***ff*** means: (5)

up to the end   held back   very loud

con moto means: means:

with movement   slight pressure

7 Music in Context /5

7.1 FALSE (1)

7.2 bar 4 (1)

7.3 (a) D (3)

    (b) bar 7

    (c) bar 4

Music Theory Practice Paper 2021 Grade 2 D
Model Answers

1 Rhythm
/15

1.1 (a) 𝄵 (3)

(b) **3/4**

(c) **2/4**

1.2 (5)

(a)

(b)

(c)

(d)

(e)

1.3 (a) 12 (2)

(b) 2

1.4 (1)

1.5 (3)

✔ ✘ ✔

1.6 (1)

☐ ✔ ☐

2 Pitch /15

2.1 (a) A (b) F♯ (c) G (6)

(d) C (e) C (f) B♭

2.2 (a) (b) 𝄞 (2)

2.3 (4)

(a) (b)

(c) (d)

2.4 (a) **TRUE** (3)

(b) **FALSE**

(c) **TRUE**

3 Keys and Scales /15

3.1 (1)

3.2 (1)

3.3 (3)

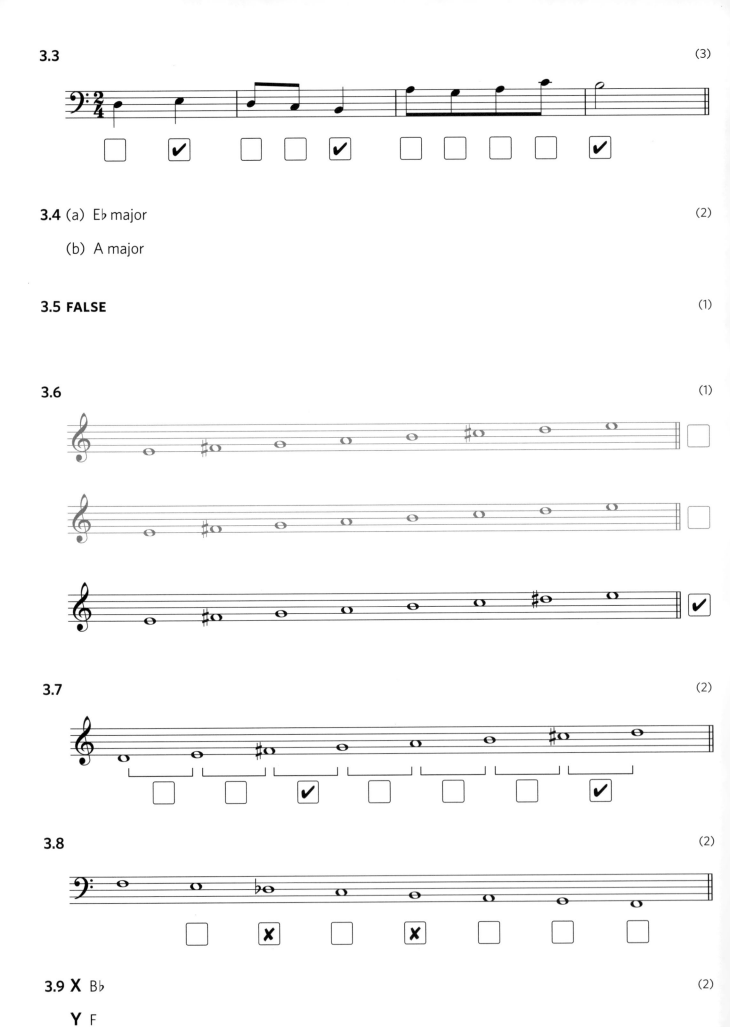

3.4 (a) E♭ major (2)

    (b) A major

3.5 FALSE (1)

3.6 (1)

3.7 (2)

3.8 (2)

3.9 X B♭ (2)

   Y F

4 Intervals

/10

(a) 2nd   (b) 7th   (c) 4th   (10)

(d) 5th   (e) 8th/8ve   (f) 3rd

(g) 2nd   (h) 6th   (i) 3rd

(j) 4th

5 Tonic Triads

/10

5.1 (a) **TRUE**   (2)

   (b) **FALSE**

5.2   (3)

      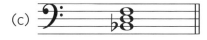

5.3 (a) D minor   (5)

   (b) A minor

   (c) E♭ major

   (d) C major

   (e) D major

6 Terms, Signs and Instruments   /5

8va------¬ means: *cantabile* means: $\overset{\wedge}{\bullet}$ $\underset{v}{\bullet}$ means: (5)

perform an octave higher   in a singing style   strong accent

Adagio means: senza means:

slow   without

7 Music in Context   /5

7.1 TRUE   (1)

7.2 3   (1)

7.3 (a) D   (3)

    (b) bar 4

    (c) bar 8